THE 50
SHADES OF BLONDE

By Stacie Harmon
Written with Jennifer Christensen
Illustrations by Doug MacGregor

ISBN: 0692471677
ISBN 13: 9780692471678

Dedicated to my mother, DeDe, and my daughter, Savannah, who together have shown me the bond that women share no matter their ages.

My mother has always encouraged me to go after my dreams, grab life by the short hairs, and hang on. Because of her, I encourage my daughter to try new things, be adventurous but cautious, and love everyone in spite of their differences. My love for them is immeasurable.

—∽—

You're at zero now. What do you have to lose?

—DeDe Miehle

ACKNOWLEDGMENTS

To Jennifer, who put her full trust in me, even when she didn't know exactly where this book was going. She's had the patience of a saint and worked diligently to quickly return fun, embellishing flavor to my stories. She has been hard at work on her own writing projects, yet still squeezed in time for mine. Thank you, Jennifer. Your contribution excites me, and opening your emails feels like opening birthday presents—so thrilling.

To Doug, who listened to me tell the stories and then put pencil to paper to make them come to life, even drawing and redrawing to make them just perfect. I feel fortunate to have such talent in my corner.

To Danette, who has several shades of blonde draping her beautiful face and came up with the cover image based on a story in the book of a woman who is so disturbed, she hacked all her hair off on her own. Brilliant work as usual, Danette. Thank you again, and congratulations on your recent nuptials!

To Laurel, who has once again nailed the editing portion of this manuscript. You've taught me to be a better writer by defining the intent and by sharing your wisdom and talent.

Heartfelt gratitude:

To my parents—all four of them—thank you for teaching me that life goes on despite divorce and that over time the heart heals and friendships with one another can bloom again.

To Savannah, my beautiful daughter, who has proved she has more depth than the ocean. Her smile shines brighter than the sun, and her calm nature challenges me to slow down and breathe, allowing for more creative tranquility.

To Maxwell, Spencer, and Paris, you all have illuminated my life. Thank you for giving me the family I've always dreamed of. The memories we've made together are forever cherished. Thank you for your support, encouragement, and sustaining love.

To my fellow stylists, you inspire me with your stories and your stamina. I know, all too well, how difficult it is to keep a smile on your face all day.

To my beloved clients, who have taught me so much about life and about myself. Through your stories I now have much more compassion and much less judgment. Thank you for your patronage and for sharing your lives with me.

A blonde walked into a hairdresser's with a pair of headphones on and asked the hairdresser for a haircut—but "don't touch the headphones, okay?"

"Fine," said the hairdresser, a little taken aback but happy for the work.

Three weeks later, the same blonde returned and asked for another haircut but with the same condition: "Whatever you do . . . don't touch the headphones."

"No problem," said the hairdresser, who went on to give her another good cut, considering the restraint.

Three weeks later, the same thing happened "and don't forget—don't touch the headphones," said the blonde. Well, just as the hairdresser was finished, she couldn't resist, and she lifted up one side of the headphones. The blonde promptly fell stone dead on the floor of the shop.

"Oh my God! I think I've killed her!" screamed the hairdresser. She picked up the headphones and put them on herself. She heard the strangest thing: "Breathe in . . . breathe out . . . breathe in . . . breathe out."

—⋙—

Hair by Stacie/The 50 Shades of Blonde

THE 50 SHADES OF BLONDE

FOREWARD

Be honest. Is there a woman out there who hasn't at least considered becoming a blonde? Even though my proud auburn locks are a part of my unique identity, there is proof in the form of a digitally modified photo that I too have entertained the idea. It's true that there are probably even more insulting blonde jokes than ginger jokes, but we certainly cannot deny the blonde allure.

The 50 Shades of Blonde is a look at the beloved blonde through the eyes of someone who perfectly embodies the old adage "blondes have more fun." Stacie Harmon's sparkling personality draws you in and makes you feel comfortable enough to share your stories—-maybe even some that might have better been kept secret.

When I met Stacie at a local event, I too was charmed by her charisma and vitality. During that first meeting, I decided to join Ninth Wave, Stacie's motivational and exciting women's group. It didn't matter that there was a chapter in Fort Myers (closer to my home); it was worth it to drive the extra miles to experience Stacie's positive energy and contagious free spirit. All these many years later, I'm proud to call her my friend.

Stacie's personal accounts and the stories revealed by her salon clients are sexy and fun. But you'll discover that just like the ever-surprising blonde herself, underneath the glitz and glam is some real insight into the world of women of all shades.

Jen Christiansen, author of *Lyla's Song*

Getting your hair done by Stacie is truly an entertaining experience. Her presence assures that there's never a dull moment as she captivates you with anecdotes of what happened yesterday or who has sauntered into the salon over the last twenty years. She's worked in some high-profile places such as MGM Grand Airline, the swanky airline to the stars, owned a trendy California salon, and is now at the beauty shop in our small town of Cape Coral.

When you're in Stacie's world, you feel like you're in an episode of *Sex and the City*! We all know which character Stacie is going to play. The only question is, which role will you, the client, choose today?

No matter what mood you're in when you enter and sit in her chair, you quickly find yourself mirroring her energy as you make sure to keep eye contact with her via the mirror in front of you. She's always got some news to share, because she doesn't let a thing around her go unnoticed.

You better be on your best behavior—but beware: something about her sparks the rebel inside of you, and you can quickly find yourself wanting to partake in the story. As you're entrusting her to make you beautiful, you can fall into the trap of wanting to bring something to the party . . . and apparently those in this book provided such spicy material. Enjoy!

Linda Hebert

PHlockers Magazine Contributor

Author of *Leaning on the Lyrics*

CHAPTER 1

The Blonde Burglar

When it comes to spotting a blonde hair on a man's coat,
every wife has 20-20 vision.
—Unknown

"All blondes are whores," said a woman seated in the hair station next to me.

I paused. Had I heard that right?

All doubt was erased when the client repeated herself; this time her teeth were clenched as her disgust and scorn reared their evil heads. "All blondes are whores!"

As if on a microphone, she attracted not only my attention, but the attention of every other stylist and client in the salon. In a domino effect, every head turned. Her stylist, Jamie, desperately tried to neutralize the situation by showing the enraged woman a new line of vibrant red color swatches.

Not allowing herself to be sidetracked, she continued her tirade. "I don't care what color you make my hair today." She dismissed the swatches with a wave of her hand. "Anything but blonde, because all blondes are whores."

Ninety-nine percent of the clients at our salon are of a cultured class, so naturally when I overheard the afflicted rage of this one-percenter next to me, I had to listen in. According to Wikipedia, "a salon is a gathering of people under the roof of an inspiring host, held partly to amuse one another and partly to refine the taste and increase the knowledge of the participants through conversation." In essence, the job of the stylist includes entertaining and increasing his or her clients' knowledge of life. I became a hairstylist because I wanted to make people beautiful, but I quickly learned that you cannot enhance people's character the same way you can enhance their appearance. Some people, as I was about to discover, are resistant to any sort of change beyond getting their hair done.

This woman was so disturbed that she either didn't notice or didn't care that there were blondes, including myself, within hearing distance of her tirade. As I weaved highlights into my client's hair, I wondered what could have made her so anti-blonde.

Glancing at the picture of my thirteen-year-old blonde daughter taped to my mirror only fed the flames of anger burning inside me. "If she says it again, I'm going to find a new use for my scissors," I stage-whispered to my client, only half-joking. I'm not normally so vindictive, but this woman was over-the-top obnoxious.

The reason behind her abrasive outbursts revealed itself over the next hour. She had caught her boyfriend cheating with a blonde.

First of all, it occurred to me that a smarter person would have taken the opposite approach and added some blonde to her chestnut strands. William Congreve must have realized something just as obvious when he wrote, "Heaven has no rage like love to hatred turned, nor hell a fury like a woman scorned." Wouldn't some flirty blonde highlights be the perfect smack in the face to the cheating boyfriend?

Secondly, it interested me that she blamed the other woman instead of her boyfriend or herself for the indiscretion. I guess it's natural to place the blame on an outside factor, in this case the blonde. It's much easier to believe that it can't be *his* fault, since that would mean he's unhappy with what she thought was a solid relationship.

Biting my tongue, I managed to keep from blurting out what was on my mind. Did the blonde tie him down and force herself upon him? Possibly it was the blonde's fault because she had a body that a porn star would envy, making it too much for a mere mortal to resist. Maybe the guilty blonde had lured him in by pulling out sex toys, lotions, and potions that this sneering woman was too intimidated to try. Had the blonde lifted her magnetic hips and drawn him to the irresistible ambrosia that moistened her vaginal lips? Did this woman envision the blonde handcuffing her boyfriend to her bed and riding him like Seabiscuit, complete with arched back and thrashing blonde hair?

Or maybe it was simply the way the blonde had looked into his eyes.

I wondered what this woman wasn't doing for him anymore that had prompted him to look elsewhere. I suppose condemning the blonde was much easier than realizing her own faults and the parts they had played in the affair.

Two months later she was back in Jamie's chair with a much different demeanor. As she asked Jamie about putting some blonde highlights in her hair, I sneaked a peek at the woman through the mirror. It was impossible not to notice the tightness of her blouse stretched over a pair of newly enhanced breasts.

So what is it about blondes? Why are they so favored and sought after? Is it truly the color of their hair or could it be more about their attitude? The European company of

Schwarzkopf, makers of one of my favorite hair color product lines, claims, "Blonde hair colours your attitude towards life. Blonde tends to make you the star wherever you go."

Clients often say that adding blonde makes them feel younger. Most say they also stand out more when they add some blonde to the mousy brown strands that make them feel like the girl next door. Those of us who are light-skinned remember that when we were children, the sun naturally lightened our virgin hair. When we get older, however, we don't have the luxury of playing on the beach or rafting in a pool. The offices we work in are usually illuminated with fluorescence that creates a mousy undertone instead of lightening and brightening our hair.

Blonde Hair Facts

- Just 2 percent of the world's population is naturally blonde.
- One of every three white females in the United States colors her hair a shade of blonde.
- Blondes are stereotyped as being youthful and sexy.
- Marilyn Monroe, who was *not* a natural blonde, refused to allow other blonde actresses on the film set with her. Her natural hair color was brown, as I am sure JFK eventually discovered.
- Barbie, a blonde, is the most popular doll in the world.

Source: facts.randomhistory.com

CHAPTER 2
The Match Dot Blonde

When I'm a blonde, I can say the world is purple and
they'll believe me because they weren't listening to me.
—Kylie Bax

During the writing of my first book, I hired a writing coach over the Internet. I was pleasantly surprised to discover it was the perfect match. Katey Coffing pushed my determination button and gave me the drive I needed to prevail—exactly what I had searched for online. Unfortunately, not everyone finds what he or she is looking for on the World Wide Web.

Several of my clients have shared stories about their Internet dates. When Internet dating began, I automatically assumed it was for the socially awkward—people who said weird things when they were nervous around the opposite sex. I'm super-outgoing, so I never knew meeting people and dating were so difficult. Since then,

I've learned that it's more often a lack of opportunity to meet someone who might be marriage material.

It seems like once the first dating site made its way to our computer screens, a thousand of them popped up. When you know exactly what or who you are looking for, I think it's a brilliant concept to be matched with someone who enjoys similar things in life. Some of my clients' stories, however, are a little more surprising than others. Carol, for example, was an attractive forty-something-year-old woman with grown children in their early twenties. She was married to the same man for twenty-two years before the D-word entered their relationship. Carol had been a schoolteacher for more than fifteen years, and it was time for her to focus on herself. I can honestly say that I applauded her courage and commended her for putting herself out there and trying Match.com, until I heard some of her stories. She told me that Dave, a firefighter, was a personal trainer on his days off from the firehouse. She showed me photos and shared what they had been talking about for about two weeks before the first date. With high anticipation of a fabulous night of "lighting the fire" between them, she wanted her hair to be perfect. I spent extra time adding three different shades of blonde to her light brown roots. Specifically brushing a lighter streak around her face, I knew she would turn his head a few times throughout the night. I couldn't wait to see her in eight weeks to hear how it had gone.

Two months later, she came in ten minutes early for her appointment and gave me the goods. "Yeah, there was no fire to put out . . ."

"What? Wait a minute," I said. "Let's get you to my chair. I'm dying to know what happened."

It was a slow day at the salon. We quickly made a beeline to my station, out of earshot of the elderly client the other stylist had in her chair. After I wrapped a smock around Carol, I leaned against my station and stood facing her. Asking about her hair would have to wait. "Okay, tell me what happened," I said.

With a chuckle over my obvious curiosity, she began. "He picked me up promptly at seven thirty, an A in my book," she said, thoughtfully turning her gold bangle bracelet back and forth around her wrist. "He arrived without flowers, but his smile made up for that. He couldn't go wrong with a blue polo shirt that showed his muscles stretching the sleeves, jeans, and worn boots."

"Sounds good so far," I said, conjuring up a yummy image of a smiling Dierks Bentley at my front door.

"Yeah, but just wait," she said, looking up at me and twisting her mouth into a sarcastic smile. "As I was admiring the way his biscuits looked in his jeans, he opened the passenger door of his Chevy Silverado. And guess what I saw?"

"Umm . . . a condom?" I blurted out. "A gun? Another woman?"

"A banana!"

"A banana? Okay . . ."

"Yes, a banana. Seeing a banana left there where I was supposed to sit—and stem side up, I'll have you know—was pretty strange."

"What did he do?" I asked, trying not to laugh.

"Well, he quickly reached in front of me to move it out of the way, but it seemed peculiar. I mean, who would not clean out their car before a first date? When I questioned him, he told me he had come straight from the gym and had forgotten to eat it between reps."

"So that was it?" I asked, reaching over for the cold, almost-forgotten coffee an earlier client had brought me.

"Yep. The date may have been the greatest date since my prom, but I couldn't get past the banana. What did it represent? Was he trying to imply something? I blew him off like a palm frond in a tropical storm. I didn't have the heart to tell him it was all because of the banana."

Whereas Carol could not move past the banana, others would have blown it off. Someone else might even have made a joke like, "I guess I have two dates tonight?" I think Carol went into her teacher mode. She assigned him an F for the banana and decided he could never recover.

Carol's story was one of many strange Internet-dating stories I've heard while standing behind the styling chair. According to the popular site Match.com, forty million Americans now use online dating, which is about 40 percent of the single population. Perhaps unsurprisingly, Statisticbrain.com says that blonde is the hair color most people are attracted to, at 32 percent. Brunettes came in second place.

Onlinedatingmagazine.com concurs; blonde women with long, straight hair have the best luck for their gender at getting dates. So off we went to color Carol's hair, so she could be matched with a guy who was not as bananas as the firefighter.

On the other hand, my regular Friday morning client, Carson, didn't believe in Internet dating. He wanted to find love in a more "natural" way, claiming he met girls easily because he was not looking—at least not in the same way as most guys. He didn't look at every woman with his tongue hanging out. Instead, he sat back and let the special ones catch his eye. Once he connected with that exceptional someone, he used his easygoing, free-spirited personality to entertain her. My favorite was the one he called the penny date. Once in the car, before he and his date pulled out of the driveway, he tossed her a penny and asked her to flip it. If it was heads, they headed left. If it was tails, they turned right. They drove that way until they spotted something worth stopping for, whether a restaurant or something to see or do. Cute, clever, unpretentious, and real. Not only did that lead him down the aisle, but they are happily married to this day.

Another client of mine, Audrey, is very humorous by nature. One day she was in my chair with her hair almost finished. She liked what she saw in the mirror, but noticed her lipstick had faded. Audrey wanted to see the final results of her hair styling with vibrant lips, so she made me wait while she pulled lip color out of her purse.

Audrey referred to her lipstick as lipdick. After I heard her say it a few times, I questioned, "Excuse me?"

"I overheard someone else call it that and thought it was so funny," she said. "It's become a horrible habit, I'll admit."

Audrey, as you can deduce by her humorous nature, had better luck in the Internet dating world.

"This style of dating opened me up to far more opportunities than I would have stumbled on if I'd waited for destiny," she said. "And although I've had a great time with everyone along the way, it's my current Internet find that captured my heart."

"Oh, congratulations," I said. "What is he like?"

"Matt is fun, silly, successful, and smart," she said. "Not to mention tall, dark-haired, and handsome, but the best part is that we don't need anything to entertain us. Wherever we are, we find something hilarious in the ordinary."

"How so?" I asked.

"Well, for example we recently watched a couple at a party. While the wife chatted, her husband checked out all the chicks. He must have been in his seventies, but I'm sure in his mind he was still twenty-five," she said with a laugh. "Matt asked me what I thought the man would say if I asked him, 'A penny for your thoughts' just as he was checking out a hot young blonde. We thoroughly entertain each other, which is key to a successful relationship. We make each other feel like there is no one else we would rather be with. And that's why we are moving in with each other."

Another client, Julie, had something else she was looking for in a relationship. She surprised me when she openly admitted that every Internet date who continued to hold her attention was rewarded with a blow job before night's end.

"I need to know how they taste before I decide to go out on a second date," she told me.

I've heard of test-driving a car before you buy it, but this was slightly more than I could wrap my head around.

It goes to show that everyone is unique when it comes to personality, values, desires, and taste. My job has certainly opened my eyes to the fact that relationships are about compatibility. No matter how attracted you are to someone, you have to be able to get along and enjoy the time spent—and, according to Julie, how they taste. I quietly thought that I needed to warn her dates not to eat asparagus.

It isn't a bad thing to question each other to figure out compatibility. Companies hiring employees do it all the time.

I found this list of online dating statistics interesting. Maybe you will too.

There are 54,250,000 single people in the United States. The number of people in the United States who have tried online dating is 41,250,000. The number of eHarmony members is 15,500,000. Match.com has 21,575,000 members. The eHarmony survey consists of 400 questions. Annual revenue from the online dating industry is $1.249 million. The average amount spent by customers on dating sites is $239. The average length of courtship for married couples who met online is 18.5 months, whereas courtship for married couples who met offline averages 42 months in length. Men make up 52.4 percent of all online dating users, and women make up 47.6

percent. Seventeen percent of the marriages in the United States in 2014 were between couples who met on a dating site. Twenty percent of current committed relationships began online. A whopping 71 percent of people believe in love at first sight. A third—33 percent—of women have sex on the first online dating encounter with someone. A bit more than half—53 percent—of people say they have dated more than one person simultaneously. Ten percent of sex offenders use online dating to meet people.

Of course by now the numbers are approximate. Below is what survey responders claimed was most important to them on a first date:

Personality 30 percent, smile and looks 23 percent, sense of humor 14 percent, career and education 10 percent

Type of hair color people are most attracted to:

Blonde 32 percent, brown 16 percent, black 16 percent, don't mind 16 percent, red 8 percent, bald 8 percent, gray 4 percent

Women's preferences:

Nice guys 38 percent, bad guys 15 percent, blend of both 34 percent, "any man I can get," 6 percent

Men's preferences:

The modern career girl 42 percent, the girl next door 34 percent, the hottie 24 percent

http://statisticbrain.com/online-dating-statistics/

CHAPTER 3

The Sugar Daddy Dream

When I'm a brunette, it's four times harder to hail a taxi. Then I go blonde again, and suddenly there are taxis everywhere.
—Sally Phillips

Melena always turned heads the moment she walked into the salon. The vibrant blonde streaks in her velvet black hair could have been the reason, but I personally believe it was the way she carried herself. Her fashion style dripped with money. I particularly admired the variety of shoes she strutted in with during her thrice-monthly visits, once to refresh her color and cut and the other two to fill her acrylic nails.

She too was a former flight attendant, so we would bat stories back and forth reliving our glory days in the sky. One day, however, she showed her true colors in a bold comment about her boyfriend.

"I absolutely despise him," she said. "I cringe when he touches me."

"Really?" I said, attempting to mask my shock. I wondered what could be so bad about him.

"Wait, let me show you a picture," she said as she rooted around in her oversized snakeskin Gucci bag.

Imagining a man as handsome as she was pretty, I nearly dropped my scissors when I saw the short, balding man smiling back from the screen of her phone. He certainly did not walk the same runway in the fashion world as Melena.

"Why do you stay with him?" I asked innocently.

"Because he pays for the lifestyle I want. It's like a job in that it pays well, but I can't stand my boss," she said. "Now that I've had a taste of this luxurious life, I can't imagine parting with it."

Revealing herself as a longtime gold-digger, she admitted that she had taken the flight attendant position not to see the world, but to work in first class so she could meet a man with money.

"My plan paid off," she continued, flashing me a self-satisfied smile in the mirror. "That's where I met Mr. Wonderful here. He travels for business constantly, which leaves me plenty of time to shop or do whatever I want. Speaking of shopping, check out the Christian Louboutin shoes I just bought. They were on sale for twenty-two hundred dollars. I'm going out with the girls this weekend and can't wait to wear them."

Dumbfounded, I asked, "Twenty-two hundred dollars? As in eleven hundred dollars each foot?"

"Yeah," she said with a giggle.

I lost count of the times Melena walked in with new shoes, probably as many times as she had been to the plastic surgeon. Liposuction, tummy tucks, boob jobs, and face-lifts. I knew because I had to be extra careful when I laid her back in the shampoo bowl. I couldn't imagine the lifestyle her doctor lived, just based on his income from her alone.

My next client, Steve, overheard our conversation while he waited. He told me he had been on a business trip with a similar type of girl. She had stopped in the Manolo Blahnik store and picked up shoes for an upcoming wedding to the tune of fifteen hundred dollars.

"They just felt soooooooo good on my feet," Steve said in the exaggerated high-pitched voice of the girl. "I told her that for that kind of money they should be giving her an orgasm with every step."

Sadly, I have found that many women share this same addiction, as another client of mine, Tom, proved when he joined an online dating website called www.sugardaddyforme.com. In most cases, this site provides dates and opportunities for successful men who don't have the time to meet decent women. From my perspective, it is a win-win situation. Like my eighty-two-year-old client Mildred always says, "You can fall in love with a rich man just like you can fall in love with a poor one."

I would never have known the sugar-daddy site was such a popular way to hook a successful man if Tom had not enlightened me after one of my jokes flopped at his next appointment. "How's that golddigger.com site working out for you, Tom?"

"It's not golddigger.com, Stacie," he said defensively. "It's Sugardaddy. Men have to prove that they make a certain amount of money to even qualify."

I wasn't sure what he meant by that, but I guess he was insisting that that made it different somehow.

Through our conversations, I grew curious about the characteristics the majority of men preferred. Most of them were looking for a woman who was . . . you guessed it, blonde! The popular site played Cupid with some of the country's richest bachelors, finding them their ideal woman: twenty-five years old, Caucasian, blonde with blue eyes, slim, and about five feet six inches tall.

I have noticed just how easy it is to fool a man. I see many women who are undeniably beautiful on the outside, but inside they are absolutely loony.

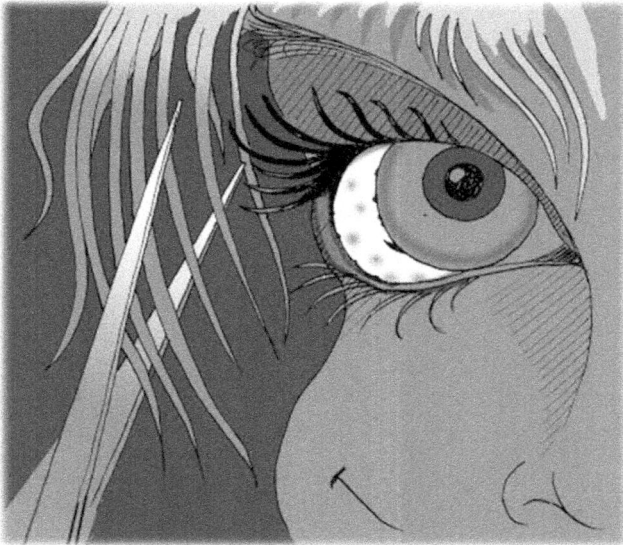

Two blondes living in Oklahoma are sitting on a bench talking when one blonde says to the other, "Which do you think is farther away . . . Florida or the moon?"

The other blonde turns and says, "Helloooooo, can you see Florida?"

CHAPTER 4
The Starry-Eyed

The best part of being blonde is forgivable momentary lapses of common sense.
—Caity Lotz

The word *lunacy* comes from the Latin word for "moon" after a correlation between the full moon and strange behaviors was noticed. Every month the lunar effect brings out the insanity in people. During one of those full moons, I met one of the strangest clients to ever sit in my chair.

This heavily accented German woman was so aggressive when making her appointment that at first I thought it was a cultural difference. She was insistent on having her hair cut on September 19.

"Are you going on a trip or something?" I asked.

"No," she said. "It is the next full moon!"

Chalking this up to bizarre eccentricity, I booked her for four o'clock on September 19. When she arrived, she told me she only wanted her tawny ends trimmed because she was growing her hair longer.

"Okay," I said. "But can you explain what you meant on the phone? About the full moon?"

"We are told to trim the ends during the full moon," she said. "Especially when the full moon is in Taurus, Cancer, Scorpio, Capricorn, or Pisces. But the best time is when the full moon is in Leo, since Leo is the sign of the lion who is born with a full, lush mane." During the short appointment, she also explained other astrology theories in detail, including those about the stars and zodiac signs.

Almost a year later, the moon incident almost forgotten, another foreign woman called for a color appointment. She asked for a specific date and quickly became annoyed that my schedule was already full on that day. With irritation in her voice, she requested an appointment a month later. Not a few days later, but an entire month later. Friday, February 14, was fully booked for Valentine's Day, so I suggested February 15.

"Not going to work," she went on. "How about March 16?"

This turned out to be a Sunday, my day off, so again I offered the day before or the next working day. Becoming even more agitated, she moved on to April 15.

That worked, so we booked it. I had no idea what her issue was until the day of her appointment. It turned out that she was another moon worshipper who believed that hair grows more slowly when the moon is in Aquarius, meaning the color would last longer.

According to a Gallup poll in 2005, only 25 percent of Americans believe in astrology, or that the position of the stars and planets affects people's lives. I'm not sure how many of them are blonde, but that would make for an interesting future study.

Q: *How can you tell which blonde is the waitress?*
A: *She is the one with the tampon behind her ear, wondering what she did with her pencil.*

CHAPTER 5

The Moody Blonde

My real hair color is kind of a dark blonde. Now I just have mood hair.
—Julia Roberts

The most perplexing problem hairdressers have is not how to hold their scissors, comb, blow-dryer, or brush. Quickly changing gears to suit the diverse personalities of their clients is what many stylists find the most challenging part of their day. We'll accept the aching legs, sore back, frequent knuckle cuts, and color-stained fingernails as part of the job, but dealing with the colorful moods our clients bring along with the picture of the celebrity they want to resemble is not taught in most cosmetology books. A university degree in psychology is what we need most. I find that after working on more women than men these days, I drink more. Just when I think I've heard it all, someone blows my mind with yet another bizarre behavior.

One client, for example, asked me to pick her hair clippings off the floor and place them in a zip-lock baggie. Certain she was going to someday have a star on Hollywood Boulevard, she wanted to save the hair for fans. I wish I could say I was kidding, but some people live in a fantasy world. Currently, she performs at our local playhouse, and I don't think she has ever been to California, let alone Hollywood.

Another client, Janine, walked into the salon shaking, her body trembling as she held a handful of her own hair. My first thought was that she was coming from a chemotherapy appointment, but as I approached her, I realized her situation was self-inflicted. Unable to get in with me for two more weeks, she had decided to take matters into her own hands. I don't mind my clients doing the occasional home bang trim, but this was indescribable. A mullet, a pixie, a bob? I'm not sure what she was going for from the looks of what was left on her head. The last time I had done her hair, I had commented that it resembled Cindy Crawford's beautiful, long, medium-brown barrel curls with various shades of blonde highlights framing her face.

On this particular day, she was broken and ready to burst into tears. She claimed that once she had started cutting, she hadn't been able to stop. It was as if she was possessed. Even her children hadn't been able to persuade her to stop.

Each child had said, "Stop, Mommy! You're going to hate it!"

She kept trimming until her oldest son yelled, "Stop, Mom! You're going to hate yourself."

At that point, she stared in the mirror and sobbed. She eventually passed out from wine and exhaustion, but a look in the mirror the next morning reminded her what she had done the night before. She had tried to fix it, but only made it worse. As a mother of five with a husband who traveled, her life was full of stress. Additionally, her husband often threatened that he wasn't happy anymore, but stayed for the sake of the kids. Her personality permanently changed when he finally told her he had fallen in love with someone else. Clearly that was traumatizing, but it was still no excuse for the way she treated me that day.

Her tone changed dramatically as she barked, "I couldn't wait another day!"

The comment in itself insinuated that I had made her do this, that it was somehow my fault. That time, however, I didn't put up with it. Before I share the reasons for quickly dismissing her, I will reveal some background about Janine.

Months earlier, Janine noticed my client Radka's striking blonde hair in the grocery store. Janine loved it so much, she questioned this perfect stranger about who did her hair. Radka, a loyal client for years, was from Slovakia. Her natural hair was a beautiful caramel brown, but she liked it heavily streaked with ash blonde. It took a long time to get it to those beautiful colors. Janine wanted her strands the exact same way and came to the salon personally to tell me. Assuming she could get an appointment at that moment was her first mistake. But because she stood there in person persuading me to stay after work, I agreed to color her that night. Janine's natural hair was twice as dark as Radka's, with warm tones.

"It will take several visits to make your hair the color of Radka's," I explained to her before beginning. "Hair color is like art to me. I need a nice canvas to work with, and then I gradually add in color. I never over-process hair."

At first, Janine seemed trusting and grateful for my concern. She looked in the mirror when I finished. "Well, it's not as blonde as I thought it would be, but it's pretty," she said.

"We need to go slow to maintain the porosity of the hair," I reminded her. "Let's meet again in three weeks for the next step."

"Okay, but I'll have to check my schedule and get back to you."

"No problem," I said. "I do book up quickly though, so please call as soon as possible."

She called in three weeks. We made an appointment for two weeks later, but she ended up going to another salon that day. The stylist attempted to bleach out all her roots, which of course turned her hair orange. Freaking out, she called me for advice.

"I can't fix it," I said. Actually it wasn't that I couldn't, but that I wouldn't. "Go back and have your natural brown put back on the roots, Janine. Then during our scheduled appointment, I'll add the highlights like we discussed."

I wasn't as perturbed as I normally would have been if a client did something like that, since I didn't know her that well. I could also tell when she asked me to stay late that she was somewhat impatient to begin with. Little did I know then that *impatient* was not the word for her; *neurotic* was a better one. I should have seen the signs, but instead I looked at those types of color jobs as career challenges that kept me sharp. When she came in that first day, impatient and demanding, I should have realized she had issues. Instead I stood at the desk listening to her go on and on about her personal life while my client Sandy sat patiently in my chair. So when the infamous mood swing incident happened, I told Janine that the problem was on the inside of her head rather than the outside. She glared at me when I suggested she go elsewhere. Afraid she might pull out a gun, I offered her the salon owner's business card.

I said, "You can call her. If she chooses to take on this beast, then so be it, but I have no more time to donate."

Out she stormed, and I haven't seen her since.

That was an extreme case of the many strange things women do involving their hair. They feel that doing something drastic to their appearance is going to change their circumstances. One client actually had a habit of singeing her hair and listening to it burn. Weird, I know. She was a smoker and tried to say that she had accidentally lit her hair on fire while lighting a cigarette, but after months of random hair breakage I knew there was more to the story. Some people with nervous tendencies twist, pull, cut, or in this case, burn their hair.

Susie, another client, often came in with the sides of her hair jacked up. She was a former hairdresser and had a pair of old shears at home in a drawer. Whenever her life got out of balance, she would start snipping the side of her hair. Always feeling as if one side was longer, she would try to even them out. By the time I saw her, she had a mullet that was longer in the back and shorter on the sides. I'm not sure if she was going for the business look in the front and a party in the back. All I know is that she showed up all jacked up.

"Did you intend to cut your sides so short?" I asked.

When the answer was no, I asked her questions and analyzed her life, again putting Psychology 101 to good use. Together we discovered that she did that only when she felt out of control. She admitted she could not control where her husband spent his late nights or where he spent their money. Her intense anxiety was taken out on her poor, defenseless hair. In this business it's a struggle not only to fix a client's hair, but to fix them.

After years of trying I now just say, "They make a drug for that!"

A blonde goes to Walmart and says to the clerk, "Hi, can I get this TV?"

Clerk: "No, we don't sell to blondes."
So the blonde goes home and dyes her hair red.
She goes to Walmart (again) and asks the clerk, "Can I get this TV?"

Clerk: "No, we don't sell to blondes."
The blonde goes home and dyes her hair brown.
She goes to Walmart (again) and asks the clerk, "Can I get this TV now!?"

Clerk: "NO! We don't sell to blondes."
This blonde won't give up, so she dyes her hair black.
She goes to Walmart (again) and asks the clerk, "Can I get this TV? That's all I want!!"

Clerk: "No, we don't sell to blondes!!!!"
So the blonde goes home and shaves her head.
She goes back to Walmart and asks the clerk, "Can I get this TV!??"
Clerk: "No, you're a blonde." The blonde, getting frustrated, asks, "Why can't I get this TV!!????"
The clerk answers, "Because this is not a TV!! It's a microwave!!!!"

A redhead tells her blonde stepsister, "I slept with a Brazilian . . ." The blonde replies, "Oh my God! You slut! How many is a Brazilian?"

CHAPTER 6
The Exhibitionist

Going blonde is like buying yourself a light bulb!
—Heidi Klum

"How much are we taking off today, Lynn? The usual?" I asked.

Instead of a typical response like "Up to my shoulders," "To chin-length," or even "To the base of my bra strap," Lynn pointed to her chest and said, "Just below the nipple."

Confused, I asked again. As she repeated herself, the man in the chair next to her straightened up like he had just received a major shot of adrenaline when he heard the word *nipple*. Isn't it strange how when men hear certain trigger words (such as *breast, nipples, lips,* or any private body part on a woman), nothing else matters?

"You know where Mark and I are going this weekend, right?" she asked.

"No," I answered, wondering if I wanted to.

"It's our anniversary, so we're going on our annual Boat in the Buff cruise to the Caribbean."

"Really? That sounds so fun," I said, mistakenly hearing "Jimmy Buffet cruise" through the noise of the blowdryer at the next station.

"So I need my ends to fall just over my nipples," Lynn continued. "Be sure you can still see the bottom of my boob."

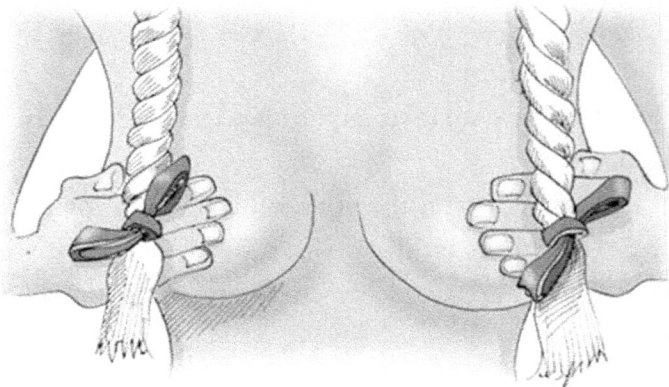

Q: *What do you call a blonde with pigtails?*
A: *A blow job with handlebars.*

Shocked by her request and wondering what it had to do with the Margaritaville king, I took my best guess. As I cut, she showed me pictures of her trip from the year before.

"Those people are naked," I said naively. "And Jimmy Buffet is performing on this ship?" I wondered if there was more to Jimmy Buffet than flip-flops and pop tops.

Lynn laughed. "Jimmy Buffet? Where'd you get that?"

"Didn't you say it was your annual Jimmy Buffet cruise?"

"No! Boat in the Buff!" She howled in hysterics before describing the journey in more detail.

Baffled, but realizing that she was entirely serious about the trip, I asked, "So, on this cruise, do you do everything naked? Eat dinner naked, too? Like at the captain's table?"

"No, silly. I'll show you what I would wear to something like that."

She showed me more photos of every outfit she planned to pack. Every photo revealed clothing that was almost completely see-through. One was mesh, the other sheer, and one just a bunch of strappy buckles.

"What about when you get to ports? What then?"

"We wear what everyone else wears. Shorts and flip-flops."

I couldn't imagine, but it turns out that there are more than enough similar people to fill a cruise ship. Fearful of asking too many questions and seeming interested in an invitation, I went back to concentrating on the haircut.

Feeling a bit curious, that night I went home to Google. Pages upon pages of clothing-optional destinations and trips popped up, as well as events in my own backyard. Well, not in *my* backyard, but certainly plenty in the area surrounding where I live. I couldn't believe that a hotel within walking distance of my house claims on their website that they cater to the *alternative* lifestyle. Before this, I probably would have thought *alternative* referred to healthy, vegan, or new age. I certainly never would have dreamed that the resort hotel and tiki hut down the street was a place to swap partners, unless you were on the dance floor.

That search ended up creating my own story to share with Lynn. When I was finished with my search on Google, my golden retriever's demanding "gotta pee" bark distracted me. I walked away from the computer without closing any of the pages. By the time my boyfriend showed up to take me to dinner, I had completely forgotten the computer and my risqué research. I thought nothing about his need to check his email on my computer before dinner. Later over plates of pasta, the dim lighting of the Italian restaurant was a blessing. An anxious flush began creeping up my neck as my boyfriend began a strange barrage of questioning.

"So, Stacie, have you ever kissed another woman?"

I nearly choked on my cappellini, since we were definitely not at that point in our relationship yet.

Uncomfortable in the silence, I blurted out, "Um . . . no, I don't play for that team. I couldn't even qualify in the LPGA."

"Okay," he said with a laugh. "I'll take that as a definite . . . maybe."

Grateful that he was amused with my joke, I thought I was free and clear. But shortly after the bus boy picked up our dinner plates, my date asked, "Have you ever seen the movie *Swingers*?"

"Hmm, yeah, I think so. A long time ago," I said, concentrating on the dessert menu. Deciding between cheesecake and crème brûlée was more on my mind than cinema. "Wasn't Vince Vaughn in that?"

He nodded. "Yeah, I think so."

I closed the menu and looked across the table at my date. "Will you split a crème brûlée with me?"

"Sure," he said, scanning the room for our waiter. "Well, what did you think about the movie?"

"What movie? Oh, *Swingers*? I don't know," I said. Now that my attention was fully on the conversation again, a little warning sound started in the back of my head. "Uh . . . just a silly comedy, I guess."

"Yeah, but the swinging thing in general. Would you ever do something like that?" His eyes darted all over the place, at the table next to us, at his dessert fork, at the ceiling light, everywhere but directly at me. And the fact that he wasn't looking at me was great, because I was wondering if I had been wrong about this guy. Was this his idea of a general tête-à-tête, or was he some sort of secret polyamorous player? As I sipped slowly on my second glass of Chianti, I wondered why all of this was coming up on the same day. My client, the Google search, and now my boyfriend?

"The only swinging I'm going to be doing is from the chandelier if we finish this bottle of wine," I joked halfheartedly. By the time dessert was served, I was fueled with liquid courage, alcohol-fueled audacity. I didn't want my curiosity about his choice of dinner conversation to gnaw away inside me. I had to be direct, so I asked him, "Is being with multiple partners something that you're into?"

"Me?" he huffed. That was when he shared his findings on my computer. Between the deep tone of his voice and questions that were laced with possible accusation, I actually felt guilty. Happy to hear the reasons and the story my client Lynn had shared, he was palpably relieved. As was I. Sharing dessert was much more fun as I retold the story.

"Oh, by the way, I did experiment with the alternative lifestyle in my late teens," I said with a sly smile. "But mostly in music."

He laughed. "Just to be clear," he said as he traced his spoon along the sides of our crème brûlée and fed it to me, "I may share my desserts, but I will never share my woman!"

Weeks later, the next time Lynn came in, I had to ask, "So how was the cruise?"

"It was an absolute blast. Met so many great people."

"And the haircut? Was it where you wanted it?"

"Oh, yes. That was perfect!" she said. "I'm sure you figured out why I wanted my hair to hit that mark."

"No, but I assumed you had a good reason," I told her. Maybe she had nipple piercings?

"I put my hair in two long ponytails in the front," she said, demonstrating by gathering her golden hair and banding it together into two sections.

"But wouldn't that shorten the hair?" I asked, curious.

"Exactly," she explained. "When I turn my head, I want the ends of my hair to brush across my nipples so they stay hard."

I was in disbelief. Not that I couldn't believe that someone would do this, but that she would be so candid.

She turned away from the mirror to look at me and said, "You know, guys bait their hook a little by ironing out the wrinkles just before they come out so their baloney pony looks at least substantial. But after a couple of drinks, their tonsil tickler shrinks up and looks like a little bag of marbles. I don't want that happening to me when I get my drink on, so my hair keeps me stimulated."

Another client, Kathy, who was sitting in the pedicure chair having her toenails coated with a summer coral polish, heard the comment about shrinking packages. She chimed in with, "My mother always referred to it as *the falling of the slop jars*. It wasn't until I became a nurse that I understood what she meant." Kathy explained that as a man ages, his twig shrinks until it's smaller than his berries.

Even though the simple fact of being blonde attracts attention, some crave even more of the limelight. Lynn was not the only flaunter. There were many others, such as Jeanie, another regular client who shared stories and pictures. She told me her husband takes her to a classy resort for couples where they hook up with anyone except their own partner. Nudity is common there on a regular basis.

I went to mix her color while Patricia, the stylist next to us, continued the conversation. As I came around the corner with bowls of color, they called me over to them. They were giggling like a couple of excited Catholic schoolgirls about to share secrets. I followed them into an empty massage room where my client nonchalantly dropped her drawers, exposing a beautiful butterfly tattooed on her vulva. It wasn't just a little cute tattoo: the entire area was covered with an ink drawing her husband had designed.

"Did it hurt?" I asked.

Q: *What did the blonde customer say to the busty waitress after reading her name tag?*

A: *"Debbie . . . That's cute. What did you name the other one?"*

"A little tender around the lips. Pinch the top of yours. Right here on the pillowy, fat tissue," she said as she demonstrated. "That part actually felt good, like acupuncture."

Patricia and I both had to admit that her taut, tan, bald beaver was beautiful, probably because Jeanie had delivered her children by Cesarean. If mine looked like that, I would want to show it off too. All I could do was stare at her vulva, a beautiful unexpected canvas. It gave me this undeniable respect for her because she was a free spirit. She believed that if it felt good, she should do it.

A blonde lost the breaststroke swimming competition. She learned later that the other swimmers had cheated; they had used their arms!!!

CHAPTER 7

The Drama Queen

*I was in love with a beautiful blonde once, dear. She drove
me to drink. That's the one thing I'm indebted to her for.*
—W.C. Fields

Forcing a smile that I hoped appeared genuine, I continued to breathe in deep, cleansing, yoga breaths. Bracing myself in preparation didn't help much as an even more dramatic, "Oh, you don't even *know*" exploded out of the Swedish blonde beneath my scissors. Everything about Anita was over the top. She gossiped about everyone, which made me wonder how she managed to keep friends. They must have enjoyed her animated facial features when she scrunched up her nose and forehead, especially when she started every sentence with, "You don't even *know!*" Needles full of Botox would be a monthly necessity if she added any more expression.

"Oh, you don't even *know*, Stacie," she said during one of her two-hour color appointments before launching into her next tirade.

Seventeen. That was the seventeenth time she had said it that day. Besides the breathing, I relied on a game of counting the number of times she repeated the phrase. It was the only way I could deal with her as she ranted on about her son's terrible teachers and criticized every messed-up relative.

"You don't even *know*! My nephew Keith? He has no clue. Instead of going to school or getting a job we can be proud of, he started playing guitar in local bars . . ."

Momentarily escaping her derogatory comments in a blissful daydream, I continued trimming. *YOU don't even know how short I can actually cut your hair! Let me show you!*

My client Nanci said it best. The way she avoids drama is to say to herself, *It's not my circus. These are not my monkeys.*

We all have someone who comes to mind when we hear the term *drama queen*. Nanci's idea of avoiding drama is a key part in living a happy life. It's easy to get dragged into someone else's drama. As women, we want to find a solution, but too often we end up becoming part of the problem. It's okay to remind ourselves that we don't have to buy into it. Once you study personalities, you will be able to quickly identify a drama queen. Ask yourself if they are a talker or a listener by nature. Are they stable or emotional, excessive or simple? I have had to learn how to be less dramatic and more peaceful. I have an expressive personality and have worked very hard to balance it. Like a peacock, I am very effusive with my emotions and want to display my variety of colors. I am social, energetic, enthusiastic, and adventurous. I love to entertain and have been told that I live every day as though it's a party. Although most people would find that lifestyle exciting, I have learned that it leads to volatile chaos if it's not balanced. I often felt I had to perform because calm and cool was boring. If I didn't feel any excitement, I would create it. It became an addiction, which could have been the cause of my devastating divorce. Since my divorce, I have decided to look deeper into who I was before the marriage. Clearly I was attracted to someone with the opposite temperament; I had no idea he was actually teaching me to be more peaceful. I thought it was corralling. Some people come into your life to calm you, whereas others feed the fire. Let's keep the drama in the world of theatrics, shall we?

Attention, all drama queens: Auditions have been canceled for today!

CHAPTER 8
The Golden Cage

Back in your gilded cage, Melanie Daniels.
—*The Birds* (1963) Director Alfred Hitchcock

I handed Maggie a cup of coffee. With her head full of foils, she continued talking.

"He keeps me in a golden cage," she said, almost as if she accepted responsibility for her husband's actions.

"What exactly does that mean?" I asked.

"He is so overprotective," she explained. "He does it out of love, I know, but I call it my golden cage."

"What kinds of things does he do?"

"Well, for instance he always says, 'Call me when you get there,'" she said with a resigned sigh. "He would have driven me here today if I hadn't insisted on driving myself. I know it's not because he thinks I'm incapable. It's just his way of showing he cares, but sometimes it seems a bit confining."

"Was he always like that?"

"Yeah, I guess so. I told him in the beginning that I was very independent, but I've learned over the years that it's just easier to appease him. Sometimes I feel anchored down by his neediness, but I know how much he adores me. That's more than I can say for most of my friends' husbands."

I nodded my head in sympathy, but secretly wondered why she would pick a man who was too suffocating for her.

"I just want to fly," she said with a dreamy expression. "Go for the day without having a plan or a time when I will return. To be so free sounds like a fantasy. I'm not saying I wish anything would happen to him, but I can tell you this: I would not marry again."

Another client, Mary, described a similar relationship with her hubby. She said he is passionate and adoring, but a bit stifling. She enjoys consignment shopping with her girlfriends, but never feels she can browse without interruption from her husband, Keith. The first call is usually because he cannot find something. The second call is always about what time he can expect her to return. He often lures her home by suggesting a favorite restaurant. Even though she would prefer to stay out and dine with friends, she gives him a time just to satisfy him.

"You learn to pick your battles," she said.

My client Annabelle argued that a woman should feel privileged if her husband wants to be with her. According to Annabelle, her first marriage was a waste. Her ex-husband would rather stay home and clean out the garage than do something she suggested. He acted as if it was an obligatory, charitable act if he accompanied her to a company Christmas party, a family member's birthday celebration, or even a neighborhood dinner party. Together they had three children and a terrific but rather sporadic sex life. "It was great," she said with a giggle, "on the three occasions I can count." She was so lonely in her marriage that when it finally dissolved, she was not even fazed.

The second time around is often a blessing.

Mary was only seventeen when she married Greg. She met him at his father's neighborhood restaurant when he was on leave from the air force. Greg was working the register the moment he first laid eyes on Mary. He said something funny that caused her to giggle, and he liked her laugh. They dated, and he quickly proposed. It was almost a year before she finally gave in and married him. He became a pilot for a commercial airline, and he also became a control freak. For example, Mary and their two daughters spent evenings at home while he was on layovers.

When he returned, she would ask to eat dinner out, but he always insisted on a home-cooked meal. After eleven years of marriage and two children, they divorced. She enjoyed her freedom, but only two months later a friend introduced her to Will at the tennis courts. Wallowing in self-pity after his wife of twenty years left him for her sister's husband, Will was not looking to meet Mary. Once introduced, however, he wanted to thank his wife for her decision. Not only was Will a gentleman, but he was funny, really funny. He was also protective and charismatic, and loved roses. They enjoyed thirty-two and a half years of blissful marriage and memories, until he complained of light-headedness and confusion. Concerned, Mary took him to the hospital, where he suffered a stroke that left him with severe dementia. Within two years, the MRIs revealed shrinkage of the hippocampus, a part of the brain associated with memory. Although Will remembered Mary, he had forgotten the most recent past. Even recognizing himself in photographs was a challenge. She sat by his bedside for six days.

"The next day was our thirty-fifth wedding anniversary," she told me. "So I purchased roses, enough roses to fill the entire hospital room. Then I read him a poem and kissed him for the final time, he passed that night."

Seeing Mary's pained expression in the mirror's reflection, I put down the scissors and squeezed her shoulder.

"I told him that I was okay with letting him go," she said, choking out the words. "I lied, I'll admit it now. I never would have been ready to let him go."

"It's been nine years since that heartbreaking day. The love he filled my heart with is what keeps me going," she said before giving me a piece of advice. "Do not marry the same type of individual the second time around. Don't make the same mistake twice."

My client Donna's story is interesting. When most of us dream about our wedding, we fantasize about our dress, our prince, the setting, and all the excitement that goes into anticipating our big day. To Donna's surprise, her experience turned out very differently.

Donna's first marriage was a mistake she would rather forget. "He was an abusive alcoholic who wouldn't let me get a job outside the house," she said as I cut her hair one day. "Instead he wanted me home making dinner, which he then wanted served hot when he came home from work. Unfortunately, too many nights his dinner sat cold on the dining room table because he had stopped for a beer on the way. One beer turned into two, two into three, and so on . . . I couldn't tell him how upset I was, because the fists would fly. I tried many times to leave, but without a job, I had no money."

Fear and a lack of education got the best of Donna, until she finally had enough courage and started applying for jobs. Home Depot accepted her application, and soon she was working four hours a day. Her husband had no idea. "He was so narcissistic, he never had a clue," Donna said. Soon she had collected enough money to hire a decent divorce attorney and serve her husband his walking papers. Now a single mother, Donna had to learn to balance work and her home life. It was difficult and exhausting, but she was proud of herself and thankful for Home Depot.

She had worked there for two years when a charming regional manager was captivated by her smile. That manager visited that store more often within the next few months than he had the entire year before. With every visit, he asked her to dinner. Donna kindly declined his invitations. She was clearly focused on her job and providing for her child. "After surviving a physically abusive relationship, the last thing anyone would want to do is jump back into a relationship of any kind, even if he was Prince Charming," she said as I combed her bangs to the side. "It took eighteen months before I finally considered it and then another two before I accepted. I have to say he was persistent. He knew I was worth his dedication." She nodded in approval of her new haircut and added, "He is the same gentleman today as he was on our first date."

One year later, he proposed—yes, right there inside Home Depot. "I was at work, and with my bright orange apron around my waist, I accepted," Donna said. "We couldn't say no when my coworkers offered to have the wedding inside the store. When I was a little girl, I dreamed of the day I would walk down the aisle, but I never imagined it would be Aisle 5 in lighting!

"We were married eight months after our engagement. My coworkers put the entire ceremony together. They created an aisle with rope lighting, dimmed the overhead chandeliers, and made my bouquet with plants and flowers from the garden department. I traded my orange apron for a beautiful white eyelet dress. The whole wedding was beautiful. We have been married for fifteen years, and I'm a firm believer in the idea that the second time around is better than the first."

As I contemplate remarrying, I've done a lot of research on the subject of second marriages.

According to the Marriage Foundation, 45 percent of marriages between first-timers are destined for the divorce courts, but just 31 percent of second weddings will end in failure. Second marriages reap the rewards of two people having survived the pain of their first marriage's ending. They never want to experience that kind of pain again, so they go into the second marriage with more maturity. The couple has usually spent a large amount of time on personal reflection, growth, healing, and change.

My client Lynette put it like this: "My second marriage works because I was really honest with myself about my role in the demise of my first marriage."

Second marriages are often happier marriages, because people have learned not to repeat their mistakes.

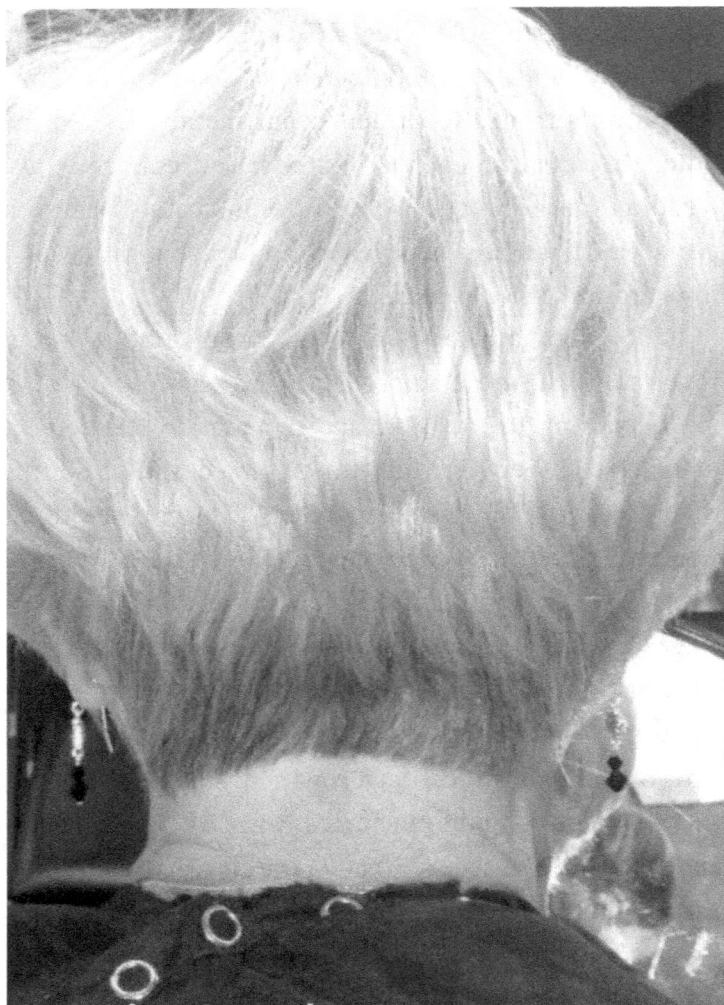

CHAPTER 9
The Bold Blonde

The world believes all blondes are stupid and brunettes are smarter. Well, I disagree.
—Anna Kournikova

The boldly self-absorbed blonde is another of my not-so-favorite clients, but as a single mother I tended to accept just about every possible appointment. Natalie, a men's rights divorce lawyer, was one of the few whom I never asked to schedule her next appointment while she was paying at the desk. I kicked myself every time, because I knew better. She always waited until the last minute and demanded an appointment, whether I had the time or not. Each time I told her I had no open slots, I had to remind her that unless she wanted to sit on another client's lap and pay for their service, she could not come in at that time. No wonder men went to her for representation; she had no problem stepping on toes to get what she wanted.

Even though I didn't possess much fondness for that type of client, it hit me that in her line of work, she may have had to wear that pushy persona to succeed. With the help of those like golden-haired Hillary Clinton, popular opinion about powerful blonde women is changing for the better. As recently as 2002, however, a survey by Clairol revealed that 76 percent of the 1,000 people surveyed thought the first female president of the United States would be a brunette. Even the successful entrepreneur of Ultimo, Michelle Mone, has claimed on social media that business blondes are not taken seriously. So perhaps Natalie had to deal with proving her strength not only as a female, but as a blonde female?

"I'm going to need a refresher on my straightening today too," Natalie said, pulling me back to the present.

"Natalie, I told you that I can't work later than six because I have to pick up my child," I said, matching her confidence.

After a brief spar during which she unsuccessfully tried to persuade me to ditch my kid and add services to her appointment, I think she discovered newfound respect for me. I wasn't going to be pushed around, and I believe she appreciated my strength and character.

It reminded me of my MGM Grand Air days and a frequent flyer the flight crew secretly called Ms. Miserable. She thought that since she produced blockbuster films and headed up a major motion picture studio, she was mightier than thou. At first I spoiled her like all of the clients, but after countless times watching her hold her bag out into the aisle until one of us would stow it for her, my desire to make her happy began to evaporate. She would see that we were busy with other passengers but had no qualms about interrupting us and asking for her bag a thousand times during the five-hour flight between New York and Los Angeles. She would take one item out of it and then hold it out again, never with a smile. We were lucky if she would even look up and acknowledge our presence. On one particular flight, I boarded early to perform my preflight safety equipment check. Suddenly I felt something warm between my legs. Yep, Aunt Flo had decided to arrive a week early. She seeped all the way through my panties and into the cotton panel of my con-trol-top nylon pantyhose. As you can imagine, I rolled my eyes. It was going to be one of those kinds of days. Needless to say I pulled out the panties I had worn the day before and the emergency pair of pantyhose I carried in case of a run and sprinted to the lavatory. Feeling not exactly fresh as a daisy, I checked the manifest of pas-sengers for the morning flight back to Los Angeles. My hopes that a favorite actor would be on it quickly dis-sipated. Not only were there no notable celebrities listed, but Ms. Miserable's name glared back at me.

"Wonderful," I said with more than a hint of sarcasm. With PMS and a slight hangover, my patience with her was gone. This time when I saw her bony arm holding the bag straight out into the aisle, I was seeing red in more ways than one.

I leaned down and said, "I am not on board to be your personal bell captain. My position is to get your ass off this jet within ninety seconds in the event of an extreme emergency."

At a loss for words, she brought the bag back to her lap.

"I'm here for your safety, princess," I continued in a calm voice. "I kindly help with your bag so you don't block the aisle for the other passengers. I need you to get whatever you need for the remainder of this flight. Then do not—I repeat, do not—ask me to get your bag or put it away again."

After that she was as sweet as peach pie. On later flights between Los Angeles and New York, she acted as if we were the best of friends, even sharing the details of films she was working on, who she had had dinner with the night before, and the best cosmetic companies.

An interesting study conducted in 2010 at the University of California, Los Angeles, found that blonde women are more aggressive and resolute about getting their way than women with other hair colors because they draw more attention and are generally viewed as more attractive. Aaron Sell, the researcher, said that this may be because blondes are so used to being treated better that they do not realize they are acting like demanding princesses. He compares it with living in a bubble. Well, this blonde was happy that she got to burst Ms. Miserable's bubble that day. As for myself, I love all the benefits of being blonde, even the assumption that I'm dumb. I live for the look in people's eyes when they realize I'm not—it is worth its weight in gold! Now I wonder about all the aspects of being blonde that I was never conscious of before. Do my brunette friends work harder and expect less special treatment than I do? Oh, there I go fanning my peacock feathers again.

They say blondes have more fun, but becoming blonde is not fun at all. Depending on the shade of natural color, it can take up to four or five treatments to get someone as blonde as they desire. Like Robyn, for example, who is of Irish descent. Even though her hair is light brown to the eye, her pigment changes fifty shades of red before it lightens to a mere orange. Sometimes the bleach needs to be reapplied with a high dose of peroxide to pass through fifty shades of yellow before settling on the pale blonde color we all know and love.

Natural blondes, found more often in northern Europe, are easier to lighten. Their hair may take one treatment. In contrast, the hair of women of Asian descent could take up to ten times to bleach out. Even after that ordeal, they may never achieve success without a toner. Explaining that to a client checking out at the cash register is anything but a field day for the stylist who stood on her feet during the entire process.

Since selling my men's salon in 2005 and choosing to work in a unisex salon, I've discovered that women are much harder to please than men. Women base their confidence on their appearance more so than men. Sitting in front of the mirror, a woman will discover at least one of her physical flaws before I can even cape her.

I've come to the conclusion that each woman is simply in a different stage of life. Everyone has a unique story. Even though we may want dissimilar things out of life, we all have the common goal of security. Each of my clients may be surfing a different wave, but they are all surfing in the same ocean. Women everywhere are searching for the wave that best suits them. Who am I to judge? Their different personalities have taught me to have more patience and recognize that I'm just as twisted as the rest. My clients have emotions that are screaming to get out, and I am no different. Sometimes I feel self-assured, confident, sophisticated, and smart. Other times I run the gamut from feeling bitter, bloated, and frumpy, to feeling sassy, sexy, assertive, dramatic, or domineering. In the blink of an eye, I can go from feeling angry, depleted, and fatigued to feeling empowered, passionate, and aggressive, or domestic, nurturing, and maternal. Sometimes I'm spiritual, grounded, and loving, but in two shakes of a lamb's tail I'm judgmental, gossipy, and shallow.

As you can see from the previous chapters, personalities are like hair. While a person may possess fifty different shades of blonde in their hair, they will also possess fifty different shades of personality. Sometimes we want to trim, color, or even cut our hair off at the root, just like we alter our moods and personality to fit an emotion.

Maybe the life of Sybil was not so far off; she's lucky she had only sixteen personalities. I feel most women, including myself, have at least fifty.

Two things define your personality: The way you manage things when you have nothing and the way you behave when you have everything.

How many characteristics do you have out of the fifty listed here?

I am the kind of person who . . .

likes to try out new activities

considers other people's feelings

has original ideas

accepts my mistakes

is modest about my achievements

is nervous before events

conceals my feelings

is critical

likes meeting new people

enjoys setting goals

follows through

feels relaxed most of the time

has a lot of energy

listens more than I talk

is comfortable being alone

can concentrate

is easily distracted

is outgoing and enthusiastic

is reserved and quiet

can multitask

is self-motivated

avoids arguments

finds it easy to compliment others

likes to argue and debate

can play an instrument

works well with others

is demanding	is more dominant
complains often	is shy
is too focused on others	seeks adventure
is indecisive	is loyal
is organized	keeps secrets
finds it easy to maintain balance	likes to travel
is a perfectionist	does yoga
hates to be late	is rebellious
is a dreamer	is obsessed with exercise
is logical	keeps a neat and tidy home
loves money more than people	is driven
always wants more	loves taking selfies

I may not have acquired a degree in psychology, but I have learned how to deal with women from all walks of life no matter their hair color. In fact, I have applied my revelations in the salon to a club I created exclusively for women called Ninth Wave. Being from California, I know that surfing is not just a sport but a way of life. It's a faith-based addiction to the idea of fearlessly jumping into uncharted waters with only a board.

Life is much like standing alone on a board in turbulent water. It's difficult to trust yourself. Having to judge just which way the tides will turn at any given moment is unnerving to say the least. All we can do is prepare ourselves with practice and perseverance. Surfing takes skill and tenacity. Only when you have taken a good hard look at yourself and understand what exactly makes you strong and unique will you be able to turn that board around and stand proud. Until we've done the inner work, we will continue to paddle through the salty white wash and hope for the best. One good ride is all it takes.

You can't stop the waves, but you can learn to surf.
—Jon Kabat-Zinn

Stacie Harmon, a full-time mother and a part-time stylist, still stands behind the chair three days a week near the gulf shores of Florida. She is the author of *Secrets Men Share When You Run Your Fingers Through Their Hair*, based on stories from the days when she owned a men's salon. She is also the founder of Ninth Wave Motivation, a women's motivational club that encourages women to step out of their comfort zones. As a former flight attendant for MGM Grand Air, her passion is to introduce her daughter to the world of travel.

Stacie would love to hear your comments.
stacieharmon9@gmail.com

www.ninthwavemotivation.com

Jennifer Christiansen is an instructor of psychology and English, holding a master of science degree in psychology and an Educational Specialist degree in higher education and adult learning. Her academic research focused on senior citizens and pet therapy. In addition to helping those with stories bring their adventures into print by serving as proofreader, editor, and ghostwriter, Jennifer enjoys writing for children and adults. She is the author of a picture book titled *Saucy's Taste of Paris* and a young adult novel called *Lyla's Song*. An active volunteer at facilities of Lee Memorial Health System, she and Heidi, one of her two miniature schnauzers, serve with Therapy Dogs, Inc. In addition to writing, teaching, and volunteering, she owns a Cruise Planners travel agency. In her free time, Jennifer reads, travels through America and Europe, and enjoys film, theater, photography, fine dining, running, agility training with her dog, and paranormal investigation. And yet, living by the beaches of Fort Myers, Florida, she still finds time for breathing the sea air and taking sandy walks with her husband and pets at sunset.

Doug MacGregor has been a cartoonist for years, getting his professional start drawing editorial cartoons for the *Norwich Bulletin* in eastern Connecticut. Eight years later he moved to Florida and began drawing for the *News Press* in Fort Myers. Doug teaches creative cartooning to the young and young at heart. He is the author of five children's books, including *Rad Hair Day* and *Get Creative: Turn on the Bright Side of Your Brain*. When Doug is not at his drawing board, you will find him singing and playing his harmonica with local blues bands.

www.dougcreates.com

NOTES

NOTES

NOTES

NOTES

NOTES

NOTES

NOTES

NOTES

NOTES